Margot Fonteyn
Rachel Stewart

Illustrated by
Linden Hamilton

Hamish Hamilton
London

Acknowledgements

The author and publisher would like to thank
Felix Fonteyn and Marguerite Porter for
their helpful comments;
also W H Allen & Co PLC for permission
to reproduce brief extracts from Margot Fonteyn's
Autobiography, © Margot Fonteyn, 1975.

HAMISH HAMILTON CHILDREN'S BOOKS

Published by the Penguin Group
27 Wrights Lane, London W8 5TZ, England
Viking Penguin Inc., 40 West 23rd Street, New York, New York 10010, U.S.A.
Penguin Books Australia Ltd, Ringwood, Victoria, Australia
Penguin Books Canada Ltd, 2801 John Street, Markham, Ontario, Canada L3R 1B4
Penguin Books (N.Z.) Ltd, 182–190 Wairau Road, Auckland 10, New Zealand

Penguin Books Ltd, Registered Offices: Harmondsworth, Middlesex, England

First published in Great Britain 1988 by
Hamish Hamilton Children's Books

Text copyright © 1988 by Rachel Stewart
Illustrations copyright © 1988 by Linden Hamilton

British Library Cataloguing in Publication Data
Stewart, Rachel
Margot Fonteyn.
1. Ballet. Fonteyn, *Dame* Margot —
Biographies — For children
I. Title   II. Series
792.8′092′4
ISBN 0-241-12506-5

Typeset by Pioneer
Printed in Great Britain by the
University Press, Cambridge

Contents

Margot Fonteyn

1   A Carefree Childhood

A small girl held her mother's hand as they walked
down a street in the London suburb of Ealing. Her
name was Peggy. She was a solemn child with straight
black hair cut in a thick fringe above large brown eyes.
She always enjoyed her mother's shopping trips,
especially when they included a search for pieces of
material to make up into costumes. Sometimes Peggy
needed these for her roles in the children's ballets that
were organised by her dancing teacher, Miss Bosustow.
At other times she simply skipped around at home
pretending to be a gypsy, a nurse, or a penguin, or
even a devil with a forked tail.

By the age of five, Peggy was making rapid progress
at Miss Bosustow's Academy and had already appeared
several times on stage. The *Middlesex County Times* of 5
July 1924 wrote appreciatively: 'In the "Silver Ballet"
there was a remarkably fine solo danced by Peggy
Hookham, which was vigorously encored.' Although
she had many other interests, she certainly took her
dancing seriously and, according to her teacher, showed
a natural grace and originality.

It was not surprising, therefore, that as she and her
mother passed the local hairdressing salon Peggy

noticed the photograph of a dancer hanging in the window. It was a playbill advertising forthcoming attractions at the Palace Theatre in the West End.

'Who is that lady?' asked Peggy curiously as she gazed at the expressive face and delicate hands.

'That is Anna Pavlova, darling, the greatest dancer in the world.'

'Then I'll be the second greatest,' replied Peggy promptly.

Her mother managed not to laugh at Peggy's lack of modesty. However, little did she realise that within twelve years, Peggy was to become known as Margot Fonteyn, the most famous ballerina Britain has ever produced.

*　　*　　*

Margaret Evelyn Hookham, called 'Peggy' by family and friends, was born on 18 May 1919 in the town of Reigate, Surrey. Peggy's father was an engineer, a kind but very practical person and a perfectionist in everything he did. He loved to solve difficult mathematical problems or tinker with machinery.

Her mother, Hilda, was quite different in temperament, impulsive and sensitive, with a natural sense of rhythm and a love of nature. She was very beautiful with dark eyes and black hair, the daughter of a Brazilian father and Irish mother. Her South American characteristics had appealed instantly to Mr Hookham. He himself had spent two wonderful years in Brazil as a boy, because his father had been sent there to manage a

Mr and Mrs Hookham

railway line. The people were so warm-hearted and their country was magnificent with its thick jungles, fine mountains and sweeping coastline.

Peggy's closest comrade was her brother Felix, just three years older than herself. She showed him utter devotion right from the very beginning, except on one terrible day when they were playing in the garden and he threw a worm at her. For several hours afterwards she didn't like Felix at all.

By that time the family had moved to Ealing and were living in a pleasant house in Elm Grove Road. On the whole the two children were moderately well behaved, kept in order by their mother's 'look', a fierce glare from her dark eyes which had a powerful intensity. They knew at once that they must do as they were told. Peggy had a stubborn streak, however, which

11

sometimes got the better of her mother, especially over the fraught question of food. There were so many items that Peggy really loathed, including milk, meat and vegetables and most especially eggs. Doughnuts, however, she adored. Sometimes when they went shopping on Ealing Broadway, Mrs Hookham would leave her daughter at Paul's Tea Shop where Peggy would eat her way through six or more. She always bit around the edge first, so that the delicious jammy centre was left till the end.

Mr Hookham asked his wife to organise deportment classes for their two children, so that they would learn to move and hold themselves correctly. Since none was available locally, Hilda took Peggy and Felix along to

Young Peggy dancing

the nearby dancing school. Grace Bosustow was a happy, encouraging person and her lessons were always well structured and enjoyable. These started with gentle exercises at the barre, based on the five positions of the feet and arms. When the children were warmed up, they were allowed to do steps in the middle of the room, until they were able to perform complete dances.

Felix really preferred to race around Ealing Common on his bicycle, while Peggy kept up as best she could. Afterwards they would stop at the shop on the corner and spend their pocket money on their favourite sweets.

For four years Peggy and Felix led a carefree existence, content in each other's company. While her brother was at school, Peggy had her lessons from a governess. Then came some devastating news. Mr Hookham had been offered the position of Chief Engineer of the British-American Tobacco Company in China. Felix, now eleven, would have to go to boarding school in England and Peggy and her mother would return from the Far East to see him only once every two years.

It was a sad little girl indeed who set sail with her parents on 5 November 1927. Muffled up in her coat and scarf, she lent over the rail of the ship and gazed with aching heart into the depths of the grey-green sea.

2 Life in the Far East

After a visit to America and several more weeks of sailing, the buildings of Shanghai finally appeared through the early morning mist. The Hookham family felt excited. As they drew closer Peggy exclaimed in astonishment: 'But China looks much more like England than America did!' Indeed, a large part of the town was European in style, although the streets were crammed with rickshaws and the busy little shops were filled with strange foods and colourful merchandise of all kinds.

The family spent a few weeks here before travelling north to their new home in the city of Tientsin. Mr Hookham's cigarette factory was nearby. A fine house was supplied by the company, with large windows and splendid pillars that supported the curving sweep of the first-floor balcony. A cook, houseboy and several other servants were already in residence.

Mrs Hookham suddenly found herself with virtually nothing to do, so she used to take her daughter across the nearby river on the ferry to the main part of town. Hilda had a soft heart and felt sorry for the caged birds and animals in the pet shops. She often took them home to care for them. Whenever Peggy wanted to

The Hookhams' home in Tientsin

practise her dancing, the rabbits, which hopped happily around the living room floor, had to be put out into the garden.

While in town they also visited the record shops and selected tuneful melodies to accompany Peggy's dancing. Peggy frequently arranged little ballets herself, all very short because the portable gramophone had to be rewound every five minutes. Her new ballet teacher was a Russian lady called Madame Tarakanova and soon Peggy was again making public performances and receiving enthusiastic reviews: 'Miss Peggy Hookham was easily the hit of the performance with her clever dancing,' wrote a local newspaper.

She attended a school for English girls in Tientsin,

but had few close friends and still missed Felix terribly. She counted the days until their return to England.

At last the time arrived and Peggy and her mother set off on the Trans-Siberian Railway through China, across Russia, then on through Germany, where they saw the magical turreted castles along the Rhine — just like Prince Siegfried's castle in *Swan Lake*. Finally they boarded the cross-Channel ferry.

During their ten-month stay in England Peggy returned to Miss Bosustow's Academy and took a ballet exam. She was especially excited when she had the opportunity to appear at the Royal Albert Hall with some other girls in a tap-dance number called 'Pickin' Cotton'. Her mother had made her a smart turquoise tunic out of velvet, decorated with gold ribbon, and matching bows for her shoes.

Their next home was to be in Hong Kong and Peggy spent an idyllic summer on the beach. She had already developed a passion for the sea and could dart in and out of the waves just like a porpoise.

Here she made a special friend, a tall handsome Norwegian diplomat called Mr Olson, who had lived in Russia before the Revolution. Peggy was spellbound as he described to her the great classical ballets he had seen there, with famous ballerinas such as Tamara Karsavina in the leading roles. He gallantly partnered the eleven-year-old Peggy at tea-dances in the Repulse Bay Hotel and they swirled around the polished floor in complete harmony.

In 1931 yet another move took the family back to Shanghai, where Mr Hookham now had a demanding senior position with his company. Regular schooling became a feature of Peggy's life and once again she was making public appearances in amateur shows. Her mother felt very proud when a photograph of Peggy portraying a Dragon Sprite was published in *The Dancing Times.*

Most importantly, Hilda had managed to track down an outstanding ballet teacher, George Gontcharov, who had trained in Russia and danced at the famous Bolshoi Theatre in Moscow. As soon as he saw Peggy, he was impressed with the beautiful way in which she held herself and with her dark, soulful eyes, capable of expressing the deep emotions of the classical ballerina roles. He agreed to teach her privately along with another English girl, June Bear, and her American friend, Virginia. Mrs Bear accompanied the trio on an ancient piano. June, who was a lovely young dancer, provided Peggy with some stiff competition, which inspired her to work twice as hard at the difficult exercises. As always, Peggy was determined to be the best in the class.

This happy life continued for two years. Then the Bears suddenly decided to leave China and take up permanent residence in London, so that June could train to be a professional dancer.

Peggy was now fourteen, and Mrs Hookham realised that they, too, had an important decision to make. If Peggy was to achieve her ambition and become another Anna Pavlova, then they hadn't a moment to lose.

3 The Making of a Ballerina

On their next leave, Mrs Hookham was determined to find the very best ballet teacher in London for Peggy. So here they were at 'The Pheasantry' in Kings Road, Chelsea, the home of the Russian Princess Serafine Astafieva. The great impresario, Serge Diaghilev, had commissioned ballets especially for her, and her former pupil, Alicia Markova, was now the star of the Vic-Wells Ballet in London.

She gazed at them gloomily down her thin, aristocratic nose. Her hair was tied up in a printed silk scarf and she carried a long cigarette holder in her elegant fingers.

'I'm too old,' she said. 'I won't take pupils more.'

Mrs Hookham pleaded: 'You must accept my daughter. I have brought her six thousand miles, all the way from China, to study with you.'

At last the princess relented and agreed to take Peggy for a class or private lesson each day. Learning with this distinguished teacher was a joy. She knew all the secrets of the most difficult techniques; steps that Peggy was unable to do before suddenly became possible.

After six months, Mrs Hookham faced another important decision. Family funds were limited and she and her daughter could not stay in London much longer unless there was an opening for Peggy in the professional ballet world. So she wrote to the Vic-Wells School for an interview. A place here would provide Peggy with the opportunity to appear with the company at Sadler's Wells Theatre. Not realising that she might be asked to do some steps, Peggy had brought no practice clothes with her, so she had to perform the audition in her bare feet and petticoat. Despite this, she was offered a place at the school, which took just eighteen girls in all.

With only two days' rehearsal, Peggy shortly found herself appearing as the third Snowflake on the left in *The Nutcracker.* 'Move right.' 'Now forward.' 'Turn.' 'Follow me,' hissed the other Snowflakes as the confused Peggy stumbled her way around the stage. Only at the very end, when imitation snow fell gently down on them in the blue light and Tchaikovsky's music rose to an inspired climax, did Peggy's spirits soar.

Within a few months she was earning a real salary — thirty shillings (£1.50) a week — as the youngest member of the *corps de ballet.* This provided a wonderful opportunity to watch her idol, Alicia Markova, rehearse and perform all the leading roles.

After the summer break, a few days spent happily camping with her mother and Felix, Peggy was amazed to see her name on the rehearsal list for a new production of *The Haunted Ballroom.* As the smallest girl in the company, she had been cast as Young Treginnis, son of the hero of the drama, who is lured to his death by ghosts. The part, although tiny, demanded considerable skill in miming, and Peggy had to open and close the ballet entirely alone on stage.

The choreography was by Ninette de Valois, their temperamental, but highly gifted Ballet Mistress who ran the company with a rod of iron. 'Will you do as I tell you!' she snapped at poor Peggy as she tried a new step. 'No! No!' banging her stick ferociously on the floor. 'Go back and do it again as I want it.' Peggy was comforted by the fact that she only shouted at dancers with talent; those without, she ignored.

A new stage name had to be found. 'Peggy Hookham' was far too plain thought Miss de Valois. So Margaret became Margot, followed by Fontes, the Brazilian family name. But her mother's relatives disapproved of

Ninette de Valois

their name being associated with the theatre. Margot looked through the telephone directory and, next to Fontes, found Fonteyn. Miss de Valois was satisfied. From now on, she would be known as Margot Fonteyn.

In 1935, aged fifteen and a half, Margot was offered her first principal role as the Creole Girl in a ballet called *Rio Grande*. She entered wholeheartedly into the spirit of the part, feeling completely at home in the South American setting. One reviewer wrote: 'Only fifteen . . . it is certain that here are the makings of a ballerina.'

The part also gave Margot the opportunity to gaze adoringly into the handsome blue eyes of her partner, William Chappell. She found him by far the kindest man in the company. The other adults at Sadler's Wells were all so witty and sophisticated that Margot could rarely understand the point of their jokes. The famous dancer Robert Helpmann was particularly awe-inspiring. She was very glad when her friend June Bear (now called Brae) joined the company.

During this year came the devastating announcement that their star, Alicia Markova, was to leave the Vic-Wells Ballet. There was no one to take her place, or so it appeared. But the far-sighted Ninette de Valois thought otherwise. Here was the opportunity for her company to produce its own ballerinas. The beautiful Pearl Argyle, who had made her name with the Ballet Rambert, took many of the leading parts, but some of Markova's roles were offered to Margot.

One was in the romantic ballet, *Les Rendezvous,* by the distinguished choreographer, Frederick Ashton, in

21

which Margot wore a most beautiful dress with a floating skirt, decorated with roses. The *Morning Post* reported that she had 'some of that intoxicating quality always associated with great dancers'. Little did they know what trouble she had had learning the part. 'Frederick Ashton is absolutely mad,' she complained to her mother. 'His steps are impossible.' He joked that her feet were so soft, they were like 'pats of butter'.

Towards the close of the 1936 season, Miss de Valois called Margot to her office. 'I'm going to give you Giselle next season; we'll start rehearsing it on the tour.' Margot gasped in astonishment. How could she possibly dance Giselle? This was one of the great romantic ballerina roles. She was far too young — only

Robert Helpmann partners Margot in her first performance of *Giselle* in 1937

seventeen. She simply wasn't ready. Doubts flooded over her as she thought of her soft feet and round face. She would let everyone down, she was sure.

Every spare moment at home was spent in the attic where she practised those tricky steps, trying to make her feet work quickly enough. Then there was the scene in which Giselle, after learning that the man she loves is already engaged to someone else, goes mad with grief. This demanded tremendous acting ability. Would she be able to do it?

On the first night, her dressing room was full of flowers and telegrams, but she was too nervous even to look at them. When at last she stepped through Giselle's cottage door on to the stage, the young girl seemed so real to Margot that she experienced every moment of Giselle's happy innocence, then her deception, her madness and finally her tragic death.

As the applause died away and the theatre emptied, Margot opened her telegrams. One of them read: 'And some have greatness thrust upon them. Good luck. De Valois.'

4 Love and War

Each year from 1936 to 1939, at the end of May, the Vic-Wells Ballet danced in Cambridge. Even though the university students were studying for important examinations, they somehow found time for innumerable parties with members of the company.

Margot shared rooms with her two friends, June Brae and Pamela May. On one evening during that first season, some students came to visit them, including two South American brothers, who performed an amazing dance with their arms outstretched, to the exotic rhythms of the rumba. Margot was entranced.

The next morning when she climbed out of bed and walked across the room, she had an extraordinary sensation. She felt as if she were floating. Then she recalled the younger of the two brothers known as 'Tito', his dark eyes, his slim figure and beautiful hands, and suddenly she realised what had happened. She was 'walking on air' — she was in love!

During that week he would appear as if from nowhere and hold Margot's hand, or sit on the floor of her dressing room and talk about his home country, Panama in Central America. At other times they would just sit or walk quietly together, knowing there was an

Tito

understanding between them that was so deep, no words could describe it.

Before sailing abroad for his vacation Tito gave her a Panamanian coin and she gave him a photograph of herself posed in a graceful arabesque, inscribed: 'For my dear Tito, from Margot'.

How she longed for a letter from him. But none came. Perhaps she had been mistaken. Perhaps he didn't really care for her. Margot thought her heart would break.

Meanwhile she was facing the greatest challenge of her career; she was to dance the dual roles of Odette

25

and Odile in *Swan Lake*. She was well suited to the part of Odette, the princess who is turned into a swan by a magician, and knew that she could portray the beautiful fluttering bird convincingly. But Odile, the magician's bewitching daughter, who deceives Prince Siegfried by pretending to be Odette, was another matter altogether. This part demanded an arrogant quality, combined with a dazzling display of technique. The notoriously difficult *fouettés* are the climax of Act III, in which the dancer spins round on one foot thirty-two times, the other never touching the floor. Margot dreaded these and she practised them over and over again. Her prince was the magnetic Robert Helpmann. Fortunately, despite his fame, he proved as before to be a most considerate partner.

The ballet was a great success and Margot's hard work was well rewarded: 'I have never seen her so regal in manner or half so brilliant,' wrote one critic. Another said, 'Last night proved that a young English dancer has genius.'

In 1939 came the terrible news that World War II had been declared. The theatre was closed and the company went on a tour of military camps. The soldiers did not always appreciate their dancing and sometimes banged their seats loudly during the performances.

Margot was concerned about her father, whom she had not seen since his last leave in 1936. Out of loyalty to his firm he had decided to stay on in China, but in 1937 the Japanese had invaded. As an enemy alien he was in considerable danger.

In May 1940 the Vic-Wells Ballet was sent to Holland

to boost the morale of the Dutch people, who faced imminent invasion by the Germans. As the dancers took their curtain calls on the opening night, the enthusiastic audience threw a shower of tulips on to the stage.

The political situation worsened during their tour and they were advised to return home sooner than planned. While staying at The Hague, they were woken up early in the morning by shouting in the hotel corridors: 'Invasion! The Germans are invading!' They

Fonteyn and Helpmann in the 1939 production of *The Sleeping Beauty*

all rushed up to the roof and saw hundreds of white blobs falling gently from the sky. German soldiers were landing by parachute near the city. Gunfire broke out and everyone scurried down to the cellars for safety.

There was a long, tense wait, while the authorities planned a way of getting them home safely. Eventually two buses with armed guards arrived. Leaving behind all their scenery, costumes and personal possessions, the dancers were driven to a quayside and crammed on board a ship with hundreds of women and children. It was nerve-racking to sit on the straw below deck, knowing that the English Channel was mined with explosives.

Five days after the company arrived home, Holland was occupied by the Germans. The dancers had been among the last people to escape.

Londoners now had to endure some terrible bombing, but despite this, the theatre was opened once again. The company's name was changed to The Sadler's Wells Ballet. In the theatre, a warning notice was displayed: 'ALERT. You will be notified by an illuminated sign if an Air Raid Warning has been sounded during the performance.' Sometimes the sign would light up and they would hear the crash of bombs and the rattle of doodlebugs getting closer, but, amazingly, not a single person ever left the theatre.

Margot's salary was now £5 per week and she and her mother moved to a pleasant house in Pelham Crescent, South Kensington. Luckily Margot was out when a flying-bomb landed across the road, killing several people and blowing out all the doors and windows of the Hookhams' home. Part of the roof fell in, too, and some ceilings came down. Miraculously Hilda was unhurt and immediately started to clean up the appalling mess.

Most of the company's male dancers were called up to join the fighting, including the talented Michael Somes. Then Frederick Ashton had to go, too. How would the company survive? Robert Helpmann, who was Australian, was fortunately able to stay on, while young students filled other roles, providing somewhat unsteady partners for the ballerinas.

Another problem was shortage of food. The dancers used up so much energy. How could they find enough to eat? It was touching when their fans brought them little parcels of rationed treats.

Meanwhile June and Pamela had both married their Cambridge boyfriends. Felix, too, found a bride and Margot sobbed at his wedding. Then the news came that their father had been put into an internment camp by the Japanese. By the end of the war she was feeling exhausted, ill and lonely. How she longed for someone to love! But her art demanded total dedication. It seemed to Margot that she was destined to remain on her own.

5 Prima Ballerina at Covent Garden

The company moved to the Royal Opera House in Covent Garden in 1946 and this raised everyone's spirits. Margot adored this historic theatre so much, she wished she could live right inside it. Instead, she bought a cosy flat just around the corner in Long Acre. The constant bustle of the fruit and vegetable market beneath her windows helped to ease her loneliness.

The good news arrived that Mr Hookham had been released from captivity. He had survived his internment by offering to help in the kitchens, which had guaranteed him a regular supply of rice.

After the horrors of war, Frederick Ashton wanted most of all to create a ballet of classic purity and the result was *Symphonic Variations,* set to César Franck's inspired music. The opening was postponed to allow Michael Somes time to recover from an injury. When the ballet was finally performed, it was hailed as a masterpiece. Most particularly it showed off the perfection of Margot's 'line', the beautiful arrangement of her limbs and angle of her head.

Despite this new success, she was still feeling exhausted. She had danced in so many ballets by now that she had a recurring nightmare that she would

The Royal Opera House, Covent Garden

forget which one she was in. She needed a break.

Taking her courage in both hands she went to see Miss de Valois and pleaded for three months leave of absence. It was granted, and Margot and her mother went to Paris. There the French dancers made a huge fuss of Margot and she became firm friends with the brilliant young choreographer, Roland Petit. He introduced her to the famous fashion designer, Christian Dior, who lent her a stunning gown to wear at an opera première.

Margot returned to London feeling revitalised. She was also looking forward, a little nervously, to working with the great Russian dancer, Léonide Massine, who was to teach the company two of his own ballets. The first was *The Three-Cornered Hat*, set to the exciting Spanish music of de Falla. Margot loved every minute of it. She danced the part of the attractive Miller's Wife and Léonide played her jealous husband. His dancing had a passionate intensity that excited audiences until they roared their approval.

Meanwhile Roland Petit had decided to create a ballet especially for Margot. She was to dance the part of Agathe, a white cat, and Roland would partner her as the young musician who falls in love with her. Agathe tries to be faithful to him, but she cannot resist the wailing of the tomcats. In the last scene she follows them on to the rooftops, chased by the young musician. At the public dress rehearsal in Paris, a terrible thing happened. As they all pounded around the tiles, the set beneath them slowly started to collapse. They sank on to the stage in a pile of splinters. There was a stunned silence as the horrified orchestra stopped playing. Margot scrambled out of the debris, took up a beautiful pose, then waved her arms at the conductor and shouted 'Play! Play!' Somehow they finished the ballet to cheers from the audience.

No ballerina, however great, can afford to stop practising. Each day she must attend class, just like the youngest pupil, and constantly refine her technique, until all the most complicated steps seem totally effortless. Margot had been thrust into leading roles when she was still a teenager. She now had the difficult task of maintaining her position as Prima Ballerina of the company.

'No ballerina, however great, can afford to stop practising.'

By a stroke of good fortune, a close friend of Margot's former teacher, George Gontcharov, came to live in London and opened a studio. Her name was Vera Volkova. She, too, had been a dancer at the Bolshoi Theatre in Moscow. Margot immediately joined her class and gradually began to absorb many subtleties of Russian interpretation and technique. Vera had a beautiful way of describing movements: 'Head is like you are smelling violets over right shoulder.' Each day Margot worked herself almost to fainting point. She knew that the critics would no longer forgive her any little mistakes.

Some fine young dancers had recently joined the company, including the lovely Violetta Elvin from Russia and the dazzling red-haired Moira Shearer. They were quickly becoming very popular with audiences.

One morning in 1948 Margot was reading the newspaper over breakfast and noticed an article about their choreographer, Frederick Ashton. His first three-act ballet, long awaited, was to be *Cinderella* and the leading role was to be shared between herself and Moira Shearer. Margot was stunned. Fred had always created new roles especially for her. Why hadn't he told her personally that she was to share this one with Moira?

She fought back the tears with difficulty as she listened to Fred's explanation. *Cinderella* was to be performed every evening at the beginning of the Christmas season, and it was too much for her to dance a three-act ballet on successive nights. Despite this reasonable explanation, Margot suddenly felt her confidence shaken to the core.

Was this why she unexpectedly lost her balance during the first night of *Don Juan* that November? As she fell, she twisted her foot very badly and had to be taken to hospital. There was no alternative but to encase her leg in plaster. In despair she travelled to Paris where Roland Petit and her other friends did their best to cheer her up. There she read of Moira Shearer's success as Cinderella. Margot was now twenty-nine. Suddenly she realised she wouldn't be able to dance for ever and that she must find new resources within herself. She took a special interest in reading, determined to catch up on her limited education.

By the end of the following February her foot had fully recovered. Then an exciting announcement was made. The Sadler's Wells Ballet was to dance at the Metropolitan Opera House in New York and *The Sleeping Beauty* was to open the season that year on 9 October with Margot in the leading role. Never before had she been so nervous for an opening night. Tragic parts suited her expressive, lyrical style of dancing well, but as Princess Aurora she had to sparkle with joy. She worried endlessly that her technique might desert her at a vital moment and that she might let the company down.

Before the curtain rose, she felt numb with fright, but as she ran on to the stage, she imagined that it really was her sixteenth birthday and the gaiety of this young princess filled her heart. Margot was radiant. Suddenly she realised that the most amazing thing was happening. The music was being drowned by applause and she had scarcely danced a step! After the Rose Adagio, the audience took to its feet and shouted its acclaim. At the end, the company had no less than twenty curtain calls.

The next day the critics were ecstatic in their praise:

'Simple and unaffected, as true greatness always is, Fonteyn knows no apparent limitation in technique'; '. . . her great elegance has never been shown to better advantage'; ' . . . a ballerina among ballerinas, tonight she conquered another continent'.

Margot sent a simple telegram to her mother: 'We seem to have made it.'

6　A Deepening Bond

After the New York season was over, the company toured the rest of North America by train, often sleeping on the way. They had a brief stop in Atlanta. Margot was unexpectedly called to the theatre manager's office because someone wished to talk to her on the telephone from New York.

'Hello, this is Tito,' said a quiet voice.

Margot's heart turned over. Tito! He was speaking as if he had seen her only yesterday, not twelve years ago. He was flying to Panama and wanted to meet her at Atlanta airport the next day. Margot was hesitant. Surely he must be married by now.

'Well, telephone me before you leave and I will go out to meet you,' she said cautiously.

The next day she waited expectantly for the call, but none came. Disappointed once more, Margot threw all her energies into her dancing.

She continued to achieve many successes and was acclaimed wherever she went. After Robert Helpmann retired, her main partner was the gallant Michael Somes. In 1951, Frederick Ashton choreographed a beautiful ballet for them, *Daphnis and Chloë,* to Ravel's enchanting music. Part of the story is portrayed on board a ship, because Chloë is captured by pirates. Margot, with her love of the sea, had an instinctive understanding of this ballet.

Her dancing was now at its peak. She was rich and famous and had many dear friends, but still her heart felt empty.

The following year in November the company toured the south of England and one morning Margot woke up feeling very feverish. She had a temperature and raging sore throat. The young doctor who came to examine her looked very concerned and injected her with the recently discovered drug, penicillin. He immediately called the ambulance. She was seriously ill with diphtheria.

A tingling sensation in her feet and tongue was followed by partial paralysis. Shortly an announcement was made in the papers that her next appearance was to be postponed 'indefinitely'. Her admirers became very alarmed. Would Margot be able to dance again?

Recovery was slow. Whenever she attempted to walk, she felt as if she were wearing lead boots, and her speech became so jumbled that people had great difficulty understanding her.

Gradually her muscles regained strength, but it was almost five months before she gave her return performance at Covent Garden in the romantic *Apparitions,* in which she appeared as the vision of a dreaming poet. At the end of the ballet, the stage was covered from wing to wing with flowers. Many people had tears streaming down their faces as they called for their favourite ballerina again and again. Feeling quite overwhelmed, Margot finally stepped forward and said, 'I don't feel I deserve any of this, but thank you, all of you, very much.'

She was deeply touched by this display of affection, but none of these people knew her personally. Their love was for Margot Fonteyn, the famous ballerina. Her life was spent mostly portraying other characters and sometimes she wondered who she herself really was.

In the autumn of 1953 the company was once again due to perform in New York. Shortly before the curtain rose, the stage doorman brought Margot a visiting card saying that the gentleman would call on her after the show. She read the card: 'Roberto E. Arias, Delegate of Panama to the United Nations'. It was Tito!

During the interval there was a knock on her dressing-room door and in walked a rather plump gentleman wearing spectacles. Was this really the same Tito that Margot had fallen in love with all those years ago? He talked with her briefly and then he was gone.

Margot was still in bed when the telephone rang the next morning. Tito announced that he was going to join her for breakfast. He sat on the floor, just as he had done in Cambridge as a student, and told her all about himself — about his marriage and his three children, and how his wife wanted to divorce him. Margot in turn explained how she never seemed able to find the right man. 'Then why don't you marry me?' said Tito. She thought this was an odd sort of a joke, but next morning an enormous basket of one hundred red roses was delivered to her room.

Soon afterwards Tito appeared again and handed

her a present. It was a sparkling diamond bracelet. 'You are going to marry me and be very happy,' he said. Margot felt hunted. She no longer knew this man, and she did not approve of divorce. But Tito was determined. He showered presents on her and took her to the most expensive restaurants. Soon he was looking thinner and happier and much more like his old self. Gradually a small corner of Margot's heart began to soften.

Tito invited a party of dancers to go for a trip on a boat belonging to his friend, the American actor John Wayne. It was a glorious day. As Margot watched the sunlight playing on the water, she came to realise that her love for Tito had renewed itself and that it was right for them to be united in marriage.

The wedding was planned for 6 February 1955, a civil ceremony to be held at the Panamanian consulate in Paris. Margot looked relaxed and happy as she arrived in her shimmering silver-grey taffeta dress, made for her by Christian Dior. But total confusion awaited her. There were so many photographers and reporters jammed into the tiny room that Margot had difficulty pushing her way through the crowd. She couldn't even see her own family. The Consul-General spoke quickly in Spanish, Tito put the wedding ring on her finger, she signed a document and it was all over.

Happily, their honeymoon made up for this somewhat unromantic wedding. They escaped to a tiny town in the Bahamas, where the local people could hardly believe their eyes. Here was the famous couple they had heard about on the radio. What a joyful welcome they gave them!

Margot and Tito on their wedding day

7   Ambassador's Wife

Not long after their marriage, Tito was appointed Panamanian Ambassador to the Court of St James's. Wearing a top hat and morning coat, he was taken in a horse-drawn carriage to the palace to present his credentials to The Queen. Margot was also allowed to attend the ceremony.

The same year, Margot had featured in the New Year's Honours List. She was to be appointed Dame of the British Empire, the youngest dancer ever to win such a title. Once again Margot was meeting royalty, this time the Queen Mother, who invested her with the order. She smiled at her warmly, congratulating her on achieving such a distinguished honour. People would now call her Dame Margot Fonteyn. She was in for a surprise, however, the next time she visited New York. The stage hands at the Metropolitan Opera House had given her the affectionate nickname of 'Dimples', which they immediately converted to 'Dame Dimples'!

As an ambassador's wife, Margot had the responsibility of running the embassy and entertaining important people from all over the world. Tito, whose father had been President of Panama, was well accustomed to State protocol, so he helped Margot with such details as making out the wine lists, choosing menus and he even advised her on what clothes she should wear. In the afternoons, Margot was expected to call on other ambassadors' wives to get to know them.

It was, of course, very difficult to fit all this in with her busy ballet schedule. In 1957 Sadler's Wells Ballet received a royal charter and was renamed The Royal Ballet. With a tour of Australia planned, Margot once again had to face being apart from Tito for some considerable length of time. Happily the Australians took Michael Somes and herself to their hearts and acclaimed their performances wherever they went. But Margot missed Tito dreadfully and secretly began to wonder whether she should retire.

As long as she was dancing in Europe, it was always possible for the two of them to snatch a weekend together now and again, or even to plan their working lives so that they could be in the same country at the same time. Once when she was dancing in Norway, Margot was deeply moved to receive amongst her fan mail a letter which said: 'I wonder can the famous Margot Fonteyn be the little Peggy I used to know in Hong Kong?' Enclosed was a snapshot inscribed, 'This is Peggy, she swims like a fish and dances like a ballerina. Summer, 1930.' There she was sitting on the beach with her charming friend, Mr Olson!

An ambassador Margot liked instantly was an energetic and humorous Brazilian. When he heard that some of Margot's ancestors were from his own country, he invited her, her mother and Tito on a wonderful holiday there.

Michael Somes and Margot in the 1958 production of Frederick Ashton's
Ondine, in which Margot danced the part of the watersprite

The highlight of the tour was a visit to the island of São Luis, birthplace of Margot's grandfather. Mrs Hookham was thrilled to be able to stand in her own father's house, an attractive Portuguese-style villa with a tiled roof. An old lady, aged ninety-eight, embraced them warmly. She had been in service with his family since she was a little girl. Margot and her mother were so moved to meet her, they could hardly drag themselves away for the rest of the tour.

Tito was frequently preoccupied with affairs in Panama. Many people were desperately poor and there were even rumours of corruption among government officials. It was said that the Chief of Police was selling surplus weapons to Colombian outlaws in return for drugs. By posing as co-pilot of a plane on a secret mission known as the 'Jungle Connection', Tito was able to witness the smuggling with his own eyes.

He was now convinced that the only way to clean up this full-scale corruption was to overthrow the government. On 24 March 1958 he resigned his post as Ambassador and started to make careful plans.

8 Revolution

Once again Margot and Michael Somes were appearing as guest artists with ballet companies the other side of the world, in Japan, then New Zealand. They danced the demanding principal roles in *Sleeping Beauty* and *Swan Lake* over and over again. Margot thought of her husband constantly. Tito was involved in secret activities in Panama and communication was very difficult.

At last she was free to join him for a holiday and Tito suggested that they go on a fishing trip. They clambered on board a small launch called *Nola*. Margot soon learnt that the real aim of the trip was to meet up with eight rebels who were hiding in the shrimp boat *Elaine*. She was extremely alarmed to hear that there was an order out for Tito's arrest. Before meeting her at the quayside, he had only just managed to dodge the police by jumping into a newspaper delivery van and hiding among the bundles of papers.

For several days Tito and Margot sailed along the coast, dropping anchor in isolated bays at night. Despite their dangerous situation, Margot felt blissfully happy. They sunbathed and swam, or just talked quietly together. It was almost like a second honeymoon.

At last they located the shrimp boat. The rebels were restless. All discussions were carried out in Spanish, so that Margot was never sure what was happening.

That night they went to look for a small speed boat that contained hidden supplies. After hours of searching, they eventually found it moored by the shore and attempted to tow it away, but it was so heavily loaded that it sank. The revolutionaries were becoming increasingly frustrated. They had to wait until darkness fell again before dragging the tiny boat on board. Working by the light of a single lamp, excitement increased as they levered up some planks that formed a false bottom. At last its deadly hoard was revealed — guns to arm the rebels.

For safety, they sailed to some uninhabited islands, where they dropped anchor. As dawn broke, Margot gasped with pleasure at the beauty of the scenery: graceful palm trees bordered the golden sands which curved around the bay.

Their tranquillity was soon to be shattered. There were shouts from the shrimp boat and the sound of a light aircraft. It was the military police — they had been discovered!

The rebels held an emergency conference and decided to try to escape by boat to Costa Rica. Meanwhile Margot was to act as a decoy by taking a long route back to the quayside in *Nola*. Then the men were gone and suddenly Margot was hit by acute despair. Perhaps they would be killed. Perhaps she would never see Tito again.

Margot gave too little thought for her own safety.

FONTEYN IN REVOLT DRAMA

The newspapers were full of Tito's revolutionary activities and Margot's exile from Panama

Back in Panama that night, her head had scarcely touched the pillow when there was a knock on the door. Margot was wanted for questioning.

She put on her clothes again and was taken by car to the Carcel Modelo, the big city gaol. The major on duty treated Margot respectfully and led her upstairs to a moderately comfortable room, clearly reserved for VIP prisoners. There was even an adjoining bathroom.

The major insisted that Margot was only a guest, but he locked the door firmly behind him. Sleep was impossible because the guards blew whistles every hour to prove that they were awake.

The following day a welcome parcel of food and clothing arrived from Tito's mother. Margot knew that she must keep a clear head for her cross-examination. She had to face this ordeal in the evening. Fortunately, she managed to convince the authorities that she had had no idea what was going on, because she spoke no Spanish. Finally the British ambassador secured her release and she was put on a plane with a one-way ticket to Miami.

It was some days before Margot received news of Tito. The shrimp boat had run short of fuel long before reaching Costa Rica, so Tito had decided to bury the arms near the coast on his father's land and seek refuge with family friends. Most of the rebels escaped to the mountains, but the military police cornered one man and shot him. A sympathetic government official concealed Tito in the boot of his car and took him to the Brazilian embassy, where he was safe. How relieved Margot was!

9 The Lion and the Lamb

Since 1954 Margot had been President of the Royal
Academy of Dancing, and one of her most important
tasks was to organise a gala each year to raise funds. A
star attraction was essential to ensure a full house.
While dancing in Russia in 1961 she had asked the
Minister of Culture if their great ballerina, Galina
Ulanova, could appear in London. Margot was deeply
disappointed, therefore, when she received a letter
some weeks later saying that Ulanova had another
engagement. Who could possibly replace her?

Then news arrived of a sensational young dancer
from the Kirov ballet company, Rudolf Nureyev, who
had recently defected to the West. He was studying in
Copenhagen with Margot's friend and former teacher,
Vera Volkova. Vera clearly thought he was a genius.
Despite his youth, Rudolf wanted to dance with Margot
herself, but she was dubious: 'Why should he decide to
dance with me when he's only twenty-three and I've
never even met him?' In the end he agreed to dance
with the American ballerina, Rosella Hightower, but
demanded a new solo for himself choreographed by
Frederick Ashton.

Margot watched the first rehearsal of this virtuoso

piece; it was called *Poème Tragique*. She had never seen anyone put so much effort and intensity into every step. Nureyev's leaps were incredible. The gala was a sell-out and Rudolf and Rosella were mobbed for autographs by the excited crowds.

Ninette de Valois decided to invite Rudolf to dance in *Giselle* at Covent Garden. 'Do you want to do it with him?' she asked Margot. Her first response was 'Oh my goodness! Don't you think I'm too old?' She discussed it with Tito.

Her husband had recently been reinstated as Ambassador to Britain and Margot was enjoying their renewed closeness. Together they came to the conclusion that Rudolf was going to be the sensation of the following year and that if Margot decided not to dance with him, she may as well consider retiring altogether. She found this new challenge impossible to resist.

When rehearsals for *Giselle* began, both Margot and Rudolf were nervous and a little wary of each other. Most of Margot's previous partners had adapted their own interpretations to suit hers, but not so Rudolf. 'Don't you think this way better?' he would say. Margot had been dancing *Giselle* for twenty-five years — since before Rudolf was born — yet she had the modesty to listen to him. She had been influenced by Russian dancers and teachers all her life and she was eager to learn how this ballet was performed by the Kirov company.

The two dancers were in fact a curious mixture of opposites. Margot was the established English ballerina who sought truthful emotional expression in all her roles, whereas Rudolf was the passionate Tartar who directed his energies through an amazing technique. They were so different in approach and temperament that critics often referred to them as 'the lion and the lamb'. Together they built up performances which on stage proved to be electrifying.

At the end of the first night of *Giselle*, as the audience clapped and roared their approval, Nureyev spontaneously fell to one knee and covered Margot's hand with kisses. She was deeply touched by this gesture and from that moment a firm bond was formed between them.

Swan Lake was their next ballet together, and once again Margot abandoned many of her steps and gestures in favour of those suggested by the young Rudolf. As usual, Margot was having trouble with the dreaded thirty-two fouettés. 'What is your mechanic for fouetté?' asked Nureyev as he watched her struggling to perfect them. But before Margot could reply he added, 'Left arm is too back.' Margot tried again and discovered to her excitement that they suddenly became easier. After their first London performance, the *Daily Mail* wrote 'She actually stopped the show with her fouettés.' Praise was lavished on them by the critics: 'A happier and more elegant combination than these two overwhelming stars is hardly thinkable,' wrote a German reviewer. The sympathy between them was so complete that the dancing seemed to 'pour from them in an unbroken stream'.

Their inspired partnership was beginning to stir the imagination of Sir Frederick Ashton, recently knighted for his outstanding contributions to British ballet. He decided to choreograph a work especially for them around the story of the 'Lady of the Camellias', a Parisian courtesan who falls in love with a young man when she is dying of consumption. Sir Frederick had heard just the right piece of music for it, an impassioned sonata by Franz Liszt. Cecil Beaton, the famous designer and photographer, was to create the costumes.

Expectations were high before the opening night of *Marguerite and Armand*, but Nureyev was suddenly taken ill and the ballet was postponed for three months. By the time it opened in March 1963, publicity had reached fever pitch. The audience was utterly enthralled with this highly charged romantic ballet, which demanded not just superb dancing, but also acting of a high order. 'An amazingly exciting work — a study in blazing emotion,' said the *Financial Times*. 'Fonteyn gives a performance of lambent (radiant) beauty that is matched by the fervour of Nureyev.'

Meanwhile, Margot's private life was once more becoming unsettled. Tito had moved their home from London back to Panama and was deeply involved in politics. He was a candidate for the National Assembly, the Panamanian parliament, and spent much time campaigning. He had been saddened by the recent death of his father and Margot longed to be able to spend more time with him. Indeed, she had again thought of retiring, but her partnership with Nureyev was now proving to be the most rewarding part of her career. Keeping up with this dynamic Tartar was taking every ounce of energy.

On 8 June 1964 Margot and Rudolf were in the city

Rudolf Nureyev and Margot Fonteyn in *Marguerite and Armand*;
'— a study in blazing emotion' was the verdict of the *Financial Times*.

of Bath rehearsing a new work, *Divertimento*, by Kenneth MacMillan. The great violinist, Yehudi Menuhin, was to play the solo violin piece by the Hungarian composer Béla Bartók, to accompany the ballet. The dancers dined late after the rehearsal and it was nearly midnight when they arrived back at the hotel. They were just climbing out of the taxi when Menuhin's wife appeared, saying anxiously, 'Tito has been shot but it is not serious, he is alive and in the hospital.' Margot felt numb. The fearful thing that she had secretly dreaded for so long had happened.

Suddenly she was overcome with terror that Tito might die. She ran down a long corridor into an empty banqueting hall and hid in a large armchair. Rudolf came to look for her and found her weeping. He put his arm round her and said that her brother-in-law was on the telephone. The line was very bad, but as far as she could tell, Tito was out of immediate danger. She promised to leave for Panama in two days, straight after the opening night of *Divertimento*.

10 Tito Fights for his Life

As Margot boarded the plane for Panama with her stepson, Roberto, she couldn't help noticing the newspaper headlines which mentioned the word 'paralysed'. She felt too stunned to tell Roberto, wanting to spare his feelings as well as her own.

The light was dimmed in the ward. Tito was lying on a narrow board. His right arm was in plaster and strapped to a stand which kept it at a right-angle. Various tubes were attached to him, mostly supplying nutrients directly into his blood stream. The worst of all was a tube that led from a hole in his throat. Tito was unable to breathe normally and the surgeon had been obliged to make this incision, so that the breath could be inhaled and exhaled directly through the windpipe. Margot realised with a terrible shock that Tito's condition was far worse than she could possibly have imagined and that he might not recover. He had in fact been shot five times at close range by a disgruntled supporter. One bullet had struck Tito at the back of his neck, causing the paralysis.

Despite Margot's fears, Tito began to recover and even regained his speech. The decision was made to send him to the Stoke Mandeville Hospital in England,

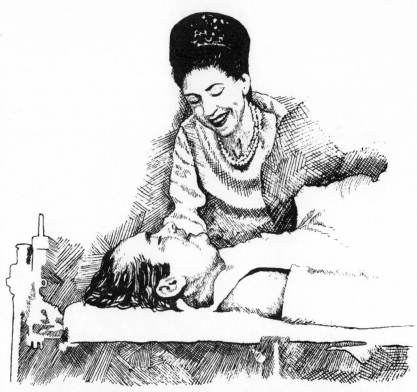

Margot comforts Tito as he is taken to Stoke Mandeville Hospital

where specialist treatment is given to patients with spinal injuries.

Margot made sure he was happily settled into the hospital, then she returned to her dancing. Now that her husband was an invalid, they would need her earnings, so any further thoughts of retirement were out of the question. Nureyev was recreating *Raymonda*, a ballet from the Russian repertoire, choreographed by Marius Petipa in 1898. It is set during the time of the Crusades. Margot found rehearsals for this three-act ballet very demanding, but she always managed to telephone Tito every morning and evening.

The première was in Italy and Margot felt lonely in the town of Spoleto. She worried endlessly about her husband. As she was putting on her make-up for the final dress rehearsal, she received an urgent message from the hospital. Tito had had a relapse. *Raymonda* was an important production for Nureyev, but despite this, he readily agreed that Margot must return to her husband.

Tito was in a coma. His heart and breathing had actually stopped after a very high fever, but, as the doctor said, they had 'pulled him back from heaven by one foot'. Once more Tito came through, but this time his speech was totally incomprehensible and his limbs were utterly useless.

It was two years before he had recovered sufficiently to leave the hospital. Even so, his speech was still unclear and he was capable only of restricted movement in his arms. Despite these severe handicaps, Tito was determined to return to politics in Panama.

An enormous crowd awaited them in his home country as he was lowered out of the plane in his wheelchair. A motorcade followed them into the city — two miles long — and thousands of well-wishers cheered them as they drove through the streets.

How proud Margot was a few days later when Tito was able to raise his own hand to make the oath required to take his place in the National Assembly! Only she knew how much courage and effort he had needed over the last two years to achieve this one small movement.

11 Many Happy Returns

In 1959 Margot had become a permanent Guest Artist of the Royal Ballet, and this allowed her to dance with different companies all over the world. Wherever she went, she always hoped that her dancing carried a message of friendship and peace.

It was on this basis that she accepted an invitation to dance in South Africa. She insisted on performing for black people as well as white, but according to the policy of apartheid the audiences were segregated. At Cape Town airport she was faced with a crowd of people carrying banners: 'Don't dance to the apartheid tune', 'Boycott in the name of human dignity'. But Margot was firm in her belief that her trip to South Africa would draw attention to the problem of apartheid.

Like Tito, she always had a deep personal concern for people suffering from poverty and hardship. A few months after dancing in the newly built theatre in the Nicaraguan capital of Managua, there was a terrible earthquake. Immediately Margot appeared on television appealing for funds to help the injured and homeless.

Margot loved to bring happiness to people through her interpretations of ballets and whenever anyone asked her about retirement she always replied, 'I see no end to my dancing.' In her mid-forties, rather than giving up the difficult classical roles, she was adding new ones to her repertoire, notably *La Sylphide*, choreographed by August Bournonville in 1836 and since made famous by the Royal Danish Ballet. It is set in Scotland and the hero is a young farmer called James. On the eve of his marriage he falls in love with the beautiful Sylph, who is a type of fairy. He tries to bind her to him for ever with a magic shawl, but as he puts it around her shoulders, her wings fall off and she dies. The tragic lyricism of this role came naturally to Margot, but she found the intricate footwork difficult to acquire. By the first night, she and Rudolf had absorbed the Danish style of dancing so completely, that no one could have guessed that they had both been brought up in totally different traditions.

In 1965, Kenneth MacMillan created his first full-length work, *Romeo and Juliet*, and Margot and Rudolf were to be the ill-fated lovers. Once again, the drama and passion of this tragic story suited them perfectly and the audience was ecstatic. Only after forty-three curtain calls were they finally allowed to go home. At the age of almost forty-six, Margot was portraying a girl thirty years younger than herself, with total conviction.

Audiences in New York loved Margot so much that they all stood up and sang 'Happy Birthday' whenever she performed at the Metropolitan Opera House on 18 May. After her fifty-third birthday performance, Clive Barnes of the *New York Times* wrote: 'She is still, without qualification, the greatest ballerina in the world. Her